IMAGES

of America

FERNDALE

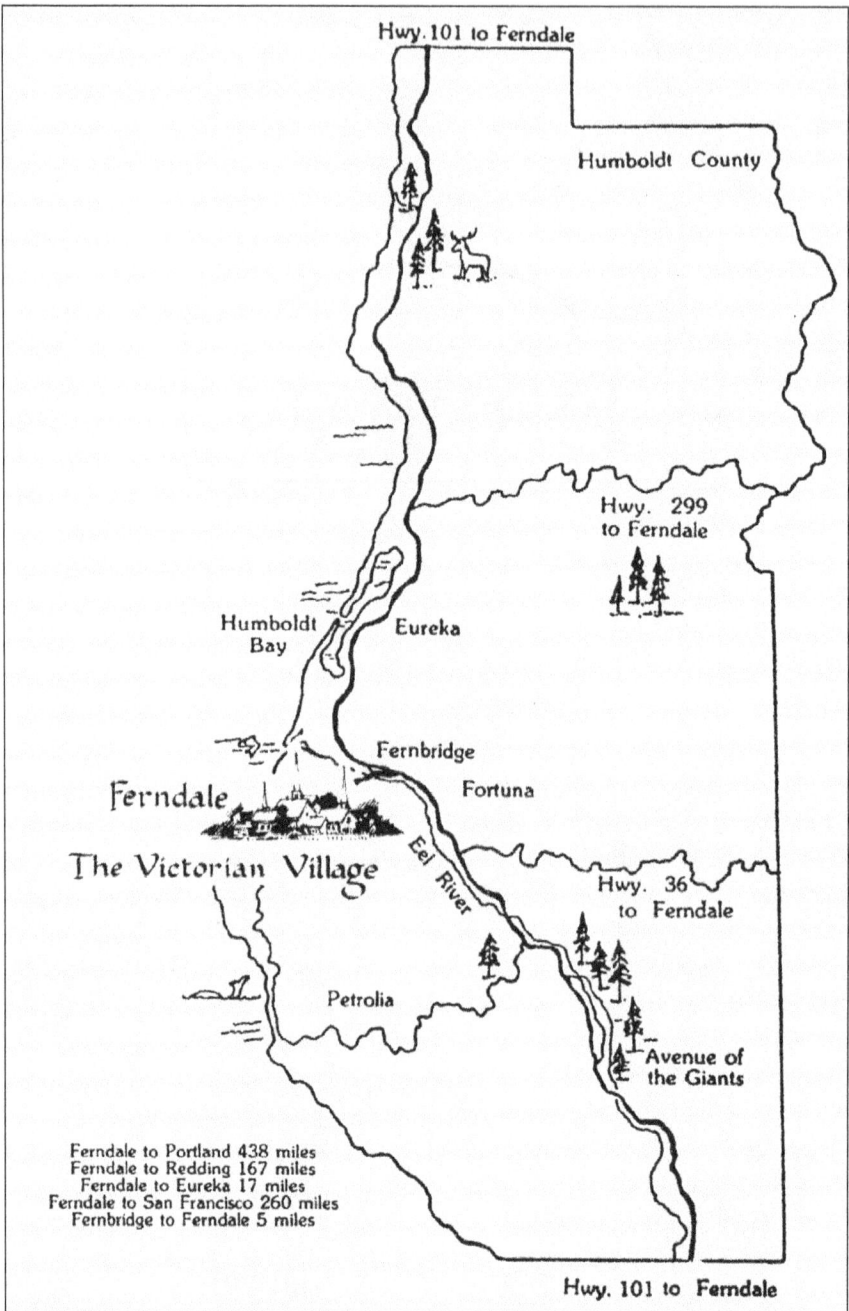

Ferndale lies south of Humboldt Bay in northern California's Humboldt County. It is halfway between the Eel River and the Pacific Ocean at latitude north 40 degrees, 35 minutes, and longitude west 124 degrees, 16 minutes. An average annual rainfall of 41 inches, dependably cool summers, and mild winters make the surrounding Eel River Valley area prime dairy country. (Courtesy of the Ferndale Chamber of Commerce, www.victorianferndale.org/chamber.)

IMAGES
of America

FERNDALE

Ferndale Museum
Carol Bess, Beryl Newman, and Ann Roberts
Editorial Committee

ARCADIA
PUBLISHING

Published by Arcadia Publishing
Charleston, South Carolina

Library of Congress Catalog Card Number: 2004104609

For all general information contact Arcadia Publishing at:
Telephone 843-853-2070
Fax 843-853-0044
E-mail sales@arcadiapublishing.com
For customer service and orders:
Toll-Free 1-888-313-2665

Visit us on the Internet at www.arcadiapublishing.com

The Ferndale Museum, 515 Shaw Avenue, P.O. Box 431, Ferndale, California 95536-0431. Telephone (707) 786-4466. E-mail: museum@quik.com.

CONTENTS

ACKNOWLEDGMENTS

The editorial committee has enjoyed working with the board of directors of the Ferndale Museum and with Jerry Lesandro, museum director, on this project. We also wish to thank Rob Roberts for his technical assistance.

Numerous local historical records, photographs, books, and other artifacts are preserved in the Ferndale Museum. It is from this material that the contents of this book have been compiled.

Thanks to the following contributors for sharing information and for supplementing our photograph collection: Denis Edeline, Joan Berman of the Humboldt Room, Humboldt State University, Trevor and Harvey Harper, and Caroline Blattner.

The employees of the Golden State Company, Ltd., plant in Ferndale show off an oversize butter carton as they sit for a photograph on August 18, 1934.

INTRODUCTION

This publication is a pictorial overview of the historical and cultural development of the "Victorian Village of Ferndale" and adjacent unincorporated areas of the Eel River Valley. It is not intended to be an exhaustive historical record. Some items otherwise worthy of inclusion have been omitted due to limitations of space.

Ferndale is a "Victorian town" in northern California's Humboldt County, 265 miles north of San Francisco. Its many colorful old buildings are preserved rather than "restored," and a number are occupied by descendants of the original owners. The city itself, incorporated in 1893, extends for only one square mile, but its postal and utility services include lands stretching to the Eel River on the north and east, Centerville and the Pacific Ocean on the west, and mountains on the south, an area colloquially referred to as "The Valley."

The Eel River Valley is alluvial and fertile land, rich with centuries of delta deposits. Prior to the incursion of white settlers, it was the home and seasonal hunting and fishing area of the semi-isolated Wiyot Indian tribe.

Euro-American settlement of this flat, thickly forested area, choked with ferns, began in 1852 when Willard Allen and Seth and Stephen Shaw paddled a borrowed Indian dugout canoe across the Eel and up Salt River to a small creek that ran through what is now Ferndale. They claimed the land at the foot of surrounding hills. That creek ran through property later acquired by pioneer Francis Francis and now bears his name.

The three men undertook the laborious work of clearing fern thickets to provide space for an access road, a cabin, and planting area. Other settlers soon followed. No fewer than ten men shared the Shaw cabin during the subsequent winter. In 1854 Seth Shaw began building a large residence and called it Fern Dale. It housed the first post office, and the town that grew up around his claim took the name for its own.

Adventurers had originally been drawn to the region during the California Gold Rush, but, finding prospecting less rewarding than they had hoped, turned to farming. Early English-speaking settlers from the United States, Britain, and Canada were joined a short time later by European immigrants from dairy-farming communities in Denmark and Switzerland. They brought their expertise and traditions of small cooperative creameries to lay the foundations of what was to become a booming industry.

By 1890 several creameries operated within a five-mile radius of Ferndale. The town was referred to as the "Cream City," and the butter produced rated best in the state. These pioneer creameries are credited with several innovations that helped transform the dairy industry. As the dairymen prospered they built large, ornate homes that became known as "Butterfat Palaces."

Portuguese, Italians, and other immigrants also settled in the area. By the last half of the 19th century Ferndale was a prosperous community and a vital transportation center. At first, cargo bound for other parts of the state was taken by wagon to Centerville Beach and loaded

7

onto ships offshore. The Salt River was navigable at that time, and in 1876, largely due to the enterprise of J.C. Kenyon, a port was constructed on the Salt River. Docks and warehouses enabled ships to sail regularly from Ferndale to San Francisco.

Ferndale was also a crossroads for stage routes running north to Eureka and south over the mountains to Bear River and Mattole. Until 1880, when Chinese labor cut the Wildcat Road from the south end of Ferndale into the hills, the last leg of the southern route followed Centerville Beach, a hazardous venture when tides were high. Coaches and carriages were quite often trapped by the tides with occasionally fatal results. Routes to the north and east were interrupted by the Eel River, and stages had to cross by ferry. When the river was low, temporary bridges could be erected, but it was not until 1911 that Fernbridge, the first permanent bridge, and at that time the world's longest reinforced concrete-arch span, was constructed.

Social and cultural activities have always centered around ethnic groups and churches. Annual festivals still reflect the town's cultural diversity. Ferndale racetrack in the northern part of town was also used for county agricultural exhibitions, and in 1896 became the permanent site of the Humboldt County Fair, which claims the record for the longest uninterrupted annual fair in California.

Cut off from the state's arterial road system by its rivers, Ferndale has avoided urban sprawl and the excessive modernization that would otherwise compromise its historical integrity. In 2002 it celebrated its sesquicentennial with an impressive display of civic and personal pride. Ferndale remains a small town with the nostalgic charm often associated with them: a place where everyone knows everyone else—usually by first name—and everyone seems related to everyone else. It is a place where neighborliness is considered less a virtue than a necessity of life.

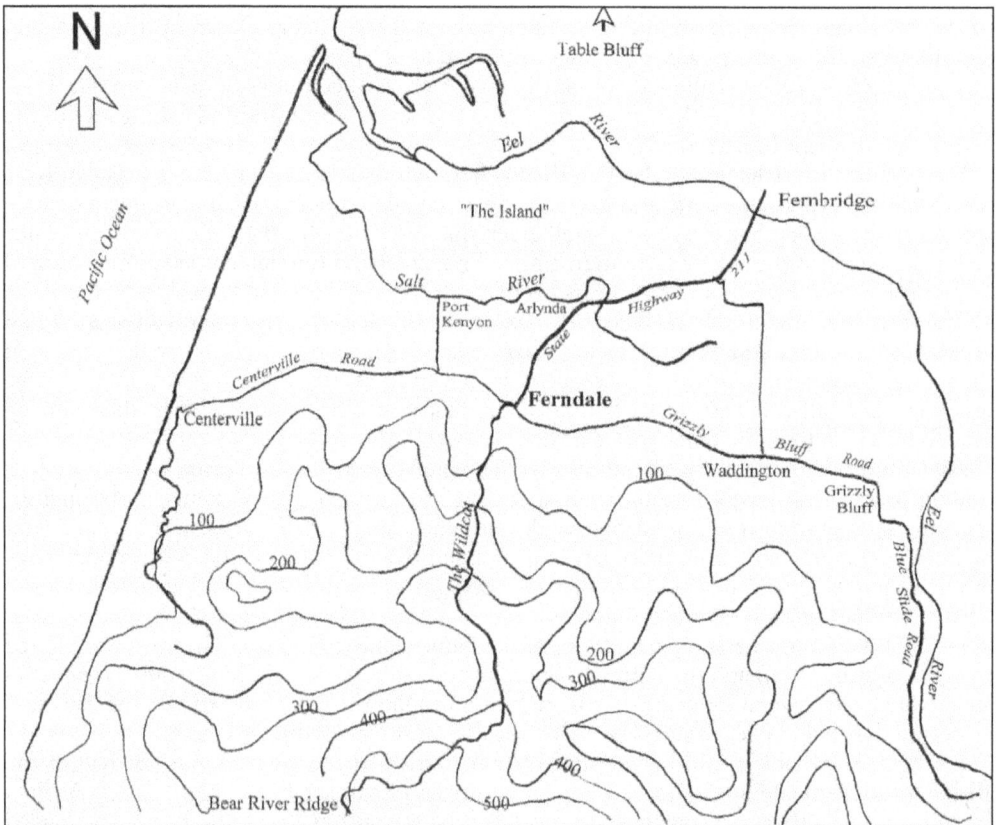

One

EARLY DAYS
IN THE VALLEY

An unknown artist sketches himself sketching the 24-year-old hamlet of Ferndale in late 1876. The Methodist Church, the Ferndale Hotel (the Ivanhoe), Dodge, Russ & Company (Valley Grocery), and the Masonic Hall can still be seen from the same vantage point today. The bare hills are now wooded and Francis Creek is obscured by buildings, but Ferndale is still known for its cows, artists, and picturesque Main Street.

Artist Stephen W. Shaw painted a portrait of Ki-we-lat-tah, Wiyot Indian leader, about 1852. Ki-we-lat-tah wears a deerskin covering and a raccoon skin on his head, and carries a fire-hardened stick, the all-purpose tool used for catching fish and to protect against bears. The artist shows a slab house with a circular door in the background and an eel basket in the foreground. Ki-we-lat-tah was nicknamed "Old Coonskin," and his descendants, some of whom are buried in the Table Bluff Cemetery north of Ferndale, are listed with Coonskin as a family name. The original portrait is on display at the Clarke Historical Museum in Eureka. (Courtesy of the Clarke Historical Museum.)

The gifts of the earth—ferns, grasses, roots, and twigs—were used to make the baskets in this Ferndale Museum display. Local Wiyot basket maker Winnie Buckley, who was born in 1876, fashioned some of the baskets and collected many of the other artifacts, including a woman's buckskin headband, hair ties used by a shaman, a smoking pipe, wrapping skin, and a gambling drum.

Seth Louis Shaw was born on a farm in Windsor, Vermont in 1816. He trained as a cabinetmaker, but eventually opened daguerreotype studios in Nashville, Tennessee and San Francisco. In 1852, he staked a claim to the quarter section of land that later became the northern half of Ferndale. Seth served his community as a farmer, land developer, postmaster, coroner, justice of the peace, California Volunteer, and founder of the local Masonic lodge. (Painting by S.W. Shaw, courtesy of Betty Genzoli.)

In 1850, Stephen William Shaw was a member of the Laura Virginia expedition to Humboldt Bay. In 1851, he spent a year at Hock Farm in the employ of John Augustus Sutter. His 1851 portrait of Sutter can be seen at the Bancroft Library at the University of California at Berkeley. Stephen returned to Humboldt County in 1852 and spent two years in agricultural labor before selling his Ferndale land claim to Francis Francis. After four years of pioneering adventures in northern California, Stephen William Shaw settled in San Francisco to begin a 50-year career as a portrait painter. (Self portrait by S.W. Shaw, courtesy of Betty Genzoli.)

11

Isabella Armitage Shaw, born in Dublin, Ireland, lived in Nashville, Tennessee as a young woman. It was there that she met daguerreotypist Seth Shaw. They were married in San Francisco in 1857, and when the couple settled in Pacific Township that year there were only two families in what is now the Ferndale city limits. Seth Shaw died in 1872, and Isabella survived him by 27 years, managing their farm and town properties.

After living in a settlers' cabin at the foot of Wildcat Road for two years, Seth Shaw began building his Gothic-style home, which he called "Fern Dale," in 1854. The house was advertised as a tavern, used as a voting place, and in 1860 served as the area's post office, thus giving the growing settlement its name, "Ferndale." Previously the region had been referred to as "Salt River," or "Pacific Township." The house is Ferndale's most prized historical and architectural treasure.

Joseph Russ came to California from Maine in 1850 and developed extensive ranching, butchering, lumber, shipping, banking, and general merchandise interests throughout Humboldt County. The noted philanthropist also served three terms in the California State Assembly, dying during his third term in 1886.

Zipporah Patrick crossed the plains in a covered wagon at the age of 13, settling with her family in Grizzly Bluff, the flatlands east of Ferndale. She became the 16-year-old bride of Joseph Russ, and raised 13 children in their rambling home, Fern Cottage, midway between Ferndale and the Pacific Ocean. After the death of her husband she continued his many enterprises under the name "Z. Russ and Sons." Ferndale's 105-acre Russ Park is Zipporah's special legacy to the town of Ferndale.

Seth Kinman was a sure shot and a mighty hunter. Upon arriving in Humboldt County in 1852, he made his living supplying elk meat to Fort Humboldt and various ships and businesses about the bay. He brought his family across the plains from Illinois in 1854, and settled into his cabin on Centerville Road in the vicinity of Fern Cottage. Later, he secured grazing land on Bear River Ridge (Kinman Pond) and farm land on Table Bluff, where he lived the rest of his life. A musician and raconteur, Seth traveled the country giving performances as a buckskin-clad character of the Far West. He designed chairs made from bearskins and elk horns, and personally presented them as gifts to Presidents Buchanan, Lincoln, Johnson, and Hayes. His fantastical chairs were put on exhibit at the Chicago World's Fair of 1893. Seth is an honorary Ferndaler because he was among the ten roaming settlers who wintered in the Shaw brothers' cabin in 1852. In 1876, he dictated his memoirs to H.H. Niebur of Ferndale. He gloried in his buckskins, was photographed in his buckskins, and was buried in his buckskins.

Francis Francis purchased Stephen Shaw's 160-acre land claim in 1856. He made excellent use of the springs in the hills on his property by establishing the Ferndale Water Works in 1875. The business became known as the Francis Land & Water Company in 1906. (Courtesy of Jim Grinsell.)

Like Ferndale pioneer women Isabella Shaw and Zipporah Russ, Grace Francis outlived her husband by a quarter of a century, taking over the family enterprise, the Ferndale Water Works, in 1877, after the death of her husband. Francis Francis, originally from Wales, came overland to California from Galena, Illinois and recommended an ocean voyage with a Panama crossing to his wife and small daughter, who would follow him. According to their accounts, both journeys, by land and by sea, were epics of hardships and aggravation.

15

Arnold Berding was a merchant in Germany, Rio de Janeiro, San Francisco, Oregon, Centerville, the Island, and finally, Ferndale, where he established the town's first general store in 1866. He stands here with his wife, Mary Wurth Blum, in front of their 1875 Gothic home on Ocean Avenue. The home, largely unchanged inside and out, is still the residence of Arnold's descendants.

Berding was not only a '49er, he was a pioneer of 1850, coming to Humboldt County in the earliest days of exploration and development on the brig *Cameo*. He was Centerville's first and only postmaster and one of Ferndale's first trustees after the vote for incorporation in 1893. Behind him stand two of the specially trimmed cypress trees that give his home its popular name, "The Gumdrop Tree House."

16

Jane Daley, who was born in Pennsylvania in 1815, married Nehemiah Patrick in 1836. In 1852, the family traveled from Illinois to California in a covered wagon.

Nehemiah Patrick was an accomplished blacksmith and orchardist. He established an early sawmill and a flour mill in the area east of Ferndale, where he owned 800 acres of land.

Grizzly Bluff, the flatlands east of Ferndale, was quickly settled with family farms. With ten rooms, two floors, and two fireplaces, the Nehemiah Patrick home, begun in 1854, still sits snugly on Grizzly Bluff Road. (Courtesy of Carol Bess.)

Uriah Williams, shown at left, and Henry S. Waterman settled on Williams Creek at about the same time the Shaw brothers made their land claims in 1852. Williams lived with his wife, Mahala Dean, and their 9 children for 50 years on his farm just east of Ferndale, raising potatoes, orchard crops, dairy cows, and blooded horses.

The Joseph Barber family purchased 360 acres in Grizzly Bluff in 1858. A son, Gardner, who inherited the property, became a county supervisor and civic leader in local church and school affairs. A second son, Charles, supervised the first phase of construction on the Wildcat Road in 1875. Gardner's mother, Nancy, cut this silhouette in Wisconsin in 1844, when he was 11 years old.

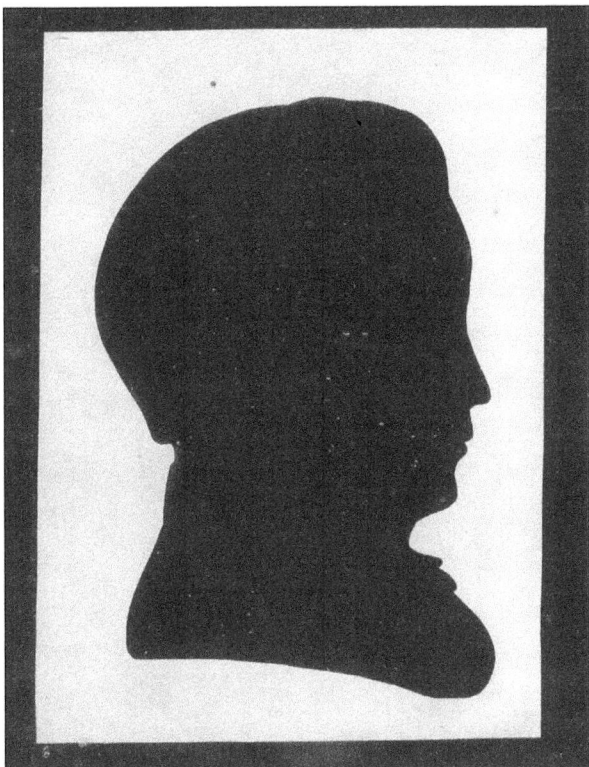

Early Ferndale farms were often extensive, with enough crops, orchards, and livestock to support a large family. Shown here is the property of Joseph and Nancy Barber.

James Smith, also known as "Gravelly," came to America from England in 1849, and purchased 160 acres of land on Centerville Road in 1858. Like pioneers Russ, Reas, Shaw, Williams, Barber, and Price, he settled on a creek that took his name. Shaw Creek, which runs from Wildcat Ridge and along Main Street to the Salt River, is known today as Francis Creek.

Jane Kent, born in Ireland, married James Smith in Wilmington, Delaware in 1852. They sailed around the Horn and lived in San Francisco for eight years before making their home to the west of the young community of Ferndale.

This view of the Ferndale Hotel at the corner of Main Street and Ocean Avenue is the earliest known photograph of Ferndale. The hotel, which was built by Frederick Cassins in about 1870, was destroyed by "the fire fiend," as the newspapers of the day put it, in September 1875, so this photograph would have been taken between those two dates. The hotel was rebuilt on similar lines and opened for business less than six months after the fire.

In 1876, inventor, investor, developer, and ventriloquist John Gardner Kenyon was ready to make his move. His lands on the bank of the Salt River, north of Ferndale, were surveyed and offered for sale.

This panoramic photograph of Ferndale in 1876 shows the scattered look of Main Street, the trees along Francis Creek, and undeveloped fields beyond the creek. It was taken some months before the sketch shown on page nine was made, because the Dodge, Russ & Company store, to the right of the Ferndale Hotel in the sketch, is not seen in this photograph. Next to the Methodist Church there are only a half dozen graves in the new Ferndale Cemetery.

Comparing the 1876 photo on the top of this page to the 1878 photo above, we notice several new homes in downtown Ferndale and several new graves in the cemetery. The most important addition to Main Street is the Russ, Searles & Putnam general store at 339 Main Street, the place to go for your groceries from that day to this.

Two

DEVELOPING
COMMUNITIES

Redwood and spruce grew in the flatlands stretching from the mountains to the Salt and Eel Rivers, as did alder, willow, and other wetland trees. The growth shown above, on the south side of the Salt River adjacent to the original Franklin Boynton property, is typical. Pioneers often cleared land back from the river banks and formed small communities and service centers to meet their most immediate needs.

The virtually impenetrable thickets of fern, growing six to eight feet high, were by far the greatest challenge to early settlers. Their formidable density can be seen in the relative heights of men and ferns in this grove.

Centerville, the terminus of an Indian trail five miles west of Ferndale on the Pacific Ocean, began in 1852 as a transportation center for off-shore shipping. Centerville Road was the first road accepted by the Humboldt County supervisors on May 1, 1855. The town included a general store, hotel, livery stable, post office, school, cooper shop, and several homes. Here we see the Julius Miranda home, which was built on the site of the old Centerville Hotel in 1891.

In 1876, John Gardner Kenyon built a wharf and warehouse on his holdings on the Salt River, establishing the first port in the valley. Salt River was navigable for five miles at that time, and steamships plying the Eureka to San Francisco route made it a regular port of call. Today the river is silted up, and little evidence of Port Kenyon's early importance remains but the name.

Looking out over the wide, green farmlands surrounding Ferndale today, it is hard to imagine the difficulties pioneers faced in their efforts to rid the area of fern thickets. Both the men and this eight-horse hauling team needed to rest from time to time during what must have been tedious and exhausting work.

Legend has it that when a steamer docked at Port Kenyon, attendance at the local school dropped dramatically as barefoot boys raced out to greet it. P.S. Inskip, the "Professor," at extreme right, was the first principal of Port Kenyon School, which opened in 1878. The old building in this photograph was replaced in 1884 by a school that was used until 1942.

44   ROBARTS BROTHERS.

W. H. ROBARTS   J. T. ROBARTS   P. W. ROBARTS   R. W. ROBARTS

ROBARTS BROTHERS
Port Kenyon, Humboldt County, Cal.

Warehousemen, Insurance Agents
AND COMMISSION MERCHANTS

AGENTS FOR

The P. C. S. S. Co's STEAMER

NEWPORT

EDWARDS   - - - -   MASTER

WILL MAKE REGULAR WEEKLY TRIPS BETWEEN

San Francisco, Shelter Cove and Port Kenyon

Leaves Port Kenyon, every Saturday Morning
Leaves San Francisco, every Wednesday Morning

——RATES OF FARE——

From Port Kenyon to San Francisco, (first class)   - - - $10.00
From Shelter Cove to San Francisco, (first class)   - -   5.00

For Freight Terms Apply to

GOODALL, PERKINS & CO.,   ROBARTS, BROTHERS
Agents No. 10 Market Street   Port Kenyon, Cala.
San Francisco, Cala.

Blue Prints, Tracing. Etc., **Maps** J. N. LENTELL, Civil Engineer
furnished on Short Notice   H St., bet, 4th and 5th, Eureka.

The four Robarts brothers, "Warehousemen, Insurance Agents, and Commission Merchants," issued this poster in 1890, giving details of rates and routes offered by the steamer *Newport*. John Kenyon started a neighboring community by moving his "Original Cheap Cash Store," built in 1879 (the first cash store in Humboldt County), one and a half miles east to Arlynda Corners. "Arlynda," from an Indian word, appropriately means "goods" or "property."

In 1875, Alexander Waddington, an Englishman, established a general store about three miles east of Ferndale and gave his name to the rural area. Waddington's children attended Coffee Creek School, named after a presumably muddy stream nearby, which may account for the number of bare feet in the front row of this school group. Waddington boasted a Literary and Debate Society, suggesting a taste for culture even in those hard days.

Named for the grizzly bears that once roamed the surrounding low hills, Grizzly Bluff, five miles from Ferndale, was a vigorous little community in the 1860s. Hot on the heels of the Petrolia oil boom, Charles and Gardner Barber drilled two wells in the area in 1864. Drilling equipment from Barber Creek can be seen in the Annex of the Ferndale Museum.

Dean's Corner, the settlement on the Centerville–Grizzly Bluff Road closest to the Eel River, was named for Henry Dean, a pioneer of 1853, shown here. Henry's son George built a school on his property in 1860, and the school was immediately offered to the local Methodist circuit rider for services. A second Grizzly Bluff School was built in 1871 by Tom Dix and J. Davenport. So, the school and church in Grizzly Bluff predated those in Ferndale by a decade.

It was fortunate for the men of the Grizzly Bluff Methodist and Presbyterian congregations that their places of worship stood in close proximity to each other. The churches shared a single organ, and four stalwarts of the faith would carry the instrument each week from one church across the road to the other, as seen here. This organ now stands in the Ferndale Museum as part of the parlor exhibit.

Ferndale's founders were English-speaking people, mainly from the United States, the United Kingdom, and Canada, but later settlers came from other parts of Europe. They added considerably to the vitality and independence that is characteristic of the region. Dairy farming, which typifies Ferndale, owes much to Danes who settled in Centerville and Port Kenyon. Julius Jacobsen, the first Danish settler in the Eel River Valley, arrived in 1873. Danish settlers founded Our Savior's Lutheran Church and co-operative creameries. Danish cultural legacy was celebrated in the annual Scandinavian Festival, with traditional outdoor dancing to ethnic music performed on the piano accordion. This gathering in Nissen's Grove on the Island is a picnic reunion of Danish residents from Ferndale and the Eel River Valley on July 12, 1895. Nissen was one of the founders of the Crown Creamery. The grove was later owned by Nissen's adopted daughter, Mrs. Minnie Frey. Below is the Danish community's entry in Ferndale's centennial parade of 1952, with Niels Lorenzen as Hans Christian Andersen.

Frank Peters, shown with his sister Maria, came from the Azores in 1879. He was the first Portuguese to settle in the area. Frank and his brothers John and William began as farm laborers. In 1888 Frank bought his own ranch and became a successful dairyman. The main influx of Portuguese began in the 1890s. They brought Old World customs and traditions with them, such as Ferndale's annual Holy Ghost Festival.

The arrival of Swiss dairy farmers more or less coincided with that of the Danes. Italians came at the turn of the century and also became involved in dairying. Among the early Italians was the DaOro family. Here Palmeira DaOro demonstrates her skill at the domestic art of spinning.

For a number of years school classes, particularly kindergarten, were held in private homes or rooms in public buildings. In 1894 Ferndale's first public kindergarten was opened in a room in the Masonic Hall. Students in this 1918 class are, from left to right, Josephine Mabry, Ralph Branstetter, Anita Parent, Gertrude Branstetter, Grace Gwendolin Shaw, their teacher Marian Osburn, Guy Maxwell, and one unidentified student. Classrooms were often sparsely furnished and basically utilitarian. The very early picture below shows a pot-bellied stove in the foreground of the room, a necessity for many months of the year, as well as an impressive pile of books on the desk. It is not clear whether the unidentified teachers are waiting for a class to arrive or relaxing after its dismissal.

The trustees of the Ferndale School District purchased a half acre of land on Ocean Avenue in 1869 for Ferndale's first school. Two small schools soon stood side by side. In 1890, a new school was constructed, also on Ocean Avenue, but it was destroyed by fire before it was ever used. The next schoolhouse, shown here, was completed in 1891, and was able to accommodate grades 1 through 10 until a high school could be built for the town. The little scholars are probably celebrating the end of the school year because this photograph was taken in June of 1893. An item in the *Ferndale Enterprise* mentions that Maynard Michel launched two tissue-paper balloons, which were inflated by burning turpentine-soaked rags. The balloons floated about a mile east to Williams Creek.

High School, Ferndale, Cal. 1963

Attempts to open a high school in Ferndale were unsuccessful prior to 1904. Two previous efforts to establish a public school brought the city council to the realization that Ferndale could support a school only in conjunction with a larger adjacent school district. In February 1907 the Ferndale Union High School was built and served the needs of the valley until 1951, when the present structure was erected.

The number of schools in the Ferndale area must say something about its residents' commitment to education. Many, like Island School, shown here, remained open until the middle of the 20th century before being absorbed into the Ferndale School District. Port Kenyon, Wildcat, Coffee Creek, Centerville, Pleasant Point, Price Creek, Bunker Hill, Grizzly Bluff, Fern Cottage, Grant, and Guthrie Schools, among others, all played an essential part in educating generations of Ferndalers.

Ferndale is a village of spires. The old Methodist Church, Our Savior's Lutheran Church, and the Congregational Church all display spires of various heights, but the Catholic Church of the Assumption, shown here, was built in 1896 and dominates the skyline with its tall silver steeple. During church renovations in 1964 the old rectory, shown in the background on the left, was sold for $1 to Viola Russ McBride, and moved to 563 Ocean Avenue to be used as a private residence.

The Methodist Church, the first church in Ferndale, built in 1873, is also graced with a fine spire. After remodeling in 1897, it was hailed as one of the most beautiful churches in the county. When the congregation merged with the Fortuna Methodist Church in 1964, the Moller pipe organ was moved to Our Savior's Lutheran Church. The building fell into disrepair until the church and the parsonage, shown to the right of the church, were restored in the 1990s as private residences.

34

Before the 1881 construction of the Congregational Church, services were held in the elementary schoolhouse. W.B. Alford, owner of the first local drug store, routinely carried chandeliers from his store for services. Joseph Russ was largely responsible for the construction of the church, donating lumber, the church bell, and one-sixth of the necessary funds.

Two sermons, one preached in Danish and the other in English, were given at the dedication of the Danish Lutheran Church with its 80-foot steeple. Now known as Our Savior's Church, it was constructed in 1899. In 1901 a parsonage was added on the corner of Fourth Street and Shaw Avenue. Originally the congregation was affiliated with the Evangelical Lutheran Church, but in 1960 it merged with the American Lutheran Church.

St. Mark's Lutheran Church (Missouri Synod), St. Mary's Episcopal Church, and the Assembly of God are apt to be overlooked by visitors, although they all have active and stable congregations and choirs. They do, however, lack spires. Church choirs like this 1899 group from the Methodist Episcopal Church, with organ pipes in the background, have always been an essential part of worship.

In 1876, the Ferndale Cemetery Association bought five acres of land on what is now Ocean Avenue from Francis and Grace Francis to begin the first town cemetery. Earlier residents buried their dead privately, often on their own land. Many of the remains from these burials were re-interred in the Ferndale Cemetery. There was even an early potter's field in the southern part of the cemetery for the indigent dead.

36

With clear springs on his land, Francis Francis was in an ideal position to provide Ferndale with its water supply, and in 1876 he built a reservoir on a hill near Wildcat Road and piped water to the town. His Ferndale Water Works was administered by the Francis family until 1955. It was then sold to the Citizens Utility Company.

This 1964 Francis Land & Water Company bill is also interesting because of the identity of the customer. Viola Russ McBride, descendant of Joseph Russ, was a community icon. As an artist she founded Ferndale's artist colony and as a civic leader she encouraged preservation of the Victorian city after disastrous floods, going so far as to buy several historic properties to prevent their destruction. A plaque, set in granite in the city parking lot, honors her dedication.

For the first 30 years after its founding, Ferndale had no fire department. The raging fires in 1875 and 1882 that threatened businesses on Main Street were fought by citizen "bucket brigades." In 1882 the town purchased a used, hand-operated pumper. Fire hydrants had been installed by Francis Francis, but Ferndale's Volunteer Fire Department was not formally instituted until 1897.

The permanent home of the fire department, this building housed the town hall after the city was incorporated in 1893. In 1967 the Ferndale Village Club donated its premises on Main and Herbert Streets to the city, and the town hall relocated to that site. In 1917, the department purchased its first motorized truck. A fire alarm bell and emergency code system was set up in 1902. Today an electric siren alerts volunteers to fire and medical emergencies.

38

F. Nelson brought electric light service to the community in 1896. In 1926 Pacific Gas and Electric took control. By 1899, telephone service by Humboldt Telephone Company was well established. This view of Main Street shows unsightly electric poles and cables. In the 1970s citizens voted for electric and telephone cables to be laid underground in the downtown area.

Although Ferndale had at least one reading room prior to 1904, it was in that year that a free public library was established in the Paine Building at the corner of Washington and Main Streets. In 1908, the city received a Carnegie grant to build a permanent facility. The newly completed Ferndale Library opened in April 1910. It became a branch of the Humboldt County Library in 1915.

Ferndale was well served by Dr. F.A. Alford, its first physician, and Dr. Hogan J. Ring, seated above with his family, who practiced here for 43 years. Dr. Ring was born Haagen J. Fjorkenstad, but he took his new last name from his family estate of Ringtogen in Norway. With a Dr. Ross, he established Ferndale's first hospital at 420 Berding Street in 1891. He established a second, short-lived hospital in his large 1899 home at 400 Berding in 1921. In this family portrait, we see the doctor with his wife and children, plus his brother Ingvald, standing at left. Ingvald died tragically in the Alaskan Gold Rush. Brother Jacob Ring, standing at right, established Ring's Drug Store.

Three

AGRICULTURE AND RURAL LIFE

This 1900 photograph shows the Dillon Peacock threshing crew at work. Agriculture in the valley began with the Shaw brothers and Willard Allen, who planted fruit trees, vegetables, and potatoes. Later as more land was cleared and claimed, other farmers raised grain and potatoes, but both proved to be unprofitable. The Russ and Morrison families, among others, tried stock raising and dairying in the hills near Bear River. As the land in the valley was cleared and improved with the introduction of clover, orchard grass, and rye grasses, dairying and cattle ranching became more profitable.

Riverside Ranch is pictured here in about 1889. Originally owned by Putnam and Smith, it was leased in 1892 by Mads Madsen, who started a small creamery there and installed a ferry across the Salt River. A few years later Madsen built an electric railroad to the Eel River to more quickly transport his milk.

The J.M. Jespersen herd is shown here grazing on leased Shaw property in Ferndale about 1890. Mr. Jespersen and his wife, Augusta Holst, both from Denmark, purchased land on Russ Lane in 1897, and then farmed in the Centerville area for ten years.

Horse-drawn mowing machines cut hay and raked it into windrows. It was then compacted by a horse-powered baler and loaded onto wagons to be hauled to the barn. Loose hay, used to feed the cows in the barn, was picked up from the wagon by a fork attached to a derrick running on a track, and was then raised to the haymow. These photos were taken at Occidental Ranch in the early 1900s. Occidental Ranch was owned by Mary Russ Robarts, daughter of Joseph Russ. Her husband, James Robarts, built a creamery there by 1892 and shipped the butter to San Francisco.

C. Rasmussen's cows are shown in the corral with various outbuildings.

An unidentified herd is pictured here with farm workers, milk buckets, and outbuildings. It is typical of local ranches in the early 1900s.

Joseph Walker poses proudly here with his pigs on the Walker Ranch at Waddington around 1900. Mr. Walker was born in Switzerland in 1873, coming to Humboldt County when he was 17. He ranched at Waddington from 1900 until his retirement. His daughter, Clara Walker Peacock, now aged 102, remembers milking cows in the corral. The pigs were fed skim milk from the Eel River Creamery, seen in the background. The creamery was built in 1892 and consolidated with the Grizzly Bluff Creamery in 1908.

A group of dairymen seeking to increase their production organized the Ferndale Cow Testing Association in 1909. Their methodology included identifying the most productive cows in their herds by measuring the amount of milk given by each cow and testing the butterfat content. H.A. Tyrell, H.F. Harbers, John Trigg, and J. Nisson were the first directors. H.F. Harbers, shown here, was the first president. He was also manager of the Grizzly Bluff Creamery. The Testing Association is still an important factor in dairying today, with computer records replacing handwritten results.

Fred Wulffe, hired as the first cow tester in 1909 at a salary of $60 per month, was receiving $110 a month by 1920. He is shown with milk pails, sample bottles, and weighing, measuring, and testing implements.

In 1910, the Cow Testing Association purchased a horse and wagon for a second tester. Casper Casanova and his horse Buster traveled to the dairies to collect and test milk samples. A car replaced the horse and wagon in 1923, and testers were paid 7¢ a mile for the use of their automobiles.

46

Ben Frost, on the left, with his brother George, was listed in the 1895–1896 Humboldt County Directory as a veterinary surgeon, practicing at Grizzly Bluff. Frost introduced de-horning to the area, and traveled the West Coast doing veterinary work and freelance newspaper reporting.

Bunker Hill Creamery was owned by Joseph Russ and managed by Rageth Sutter, a Romansch Swiss, who also managed the ranch at Bunker Hill. The early small creameries on ranches in the Bear River area stored their butter in boxes and kegs and shipped it from Port Kenyon in July or September, whenever the best prices would be received.

The Grizzly Bluff Creamery, located at Grizzly Bluff and Pleasant Point Roads, was established in 1890 by Joe Davenport, its first manager. Walter Church, George Sweet, and James Lawson were also involved in establishing the creamery. G.C. Barber, James Lawson, and H.F. Harbers were later managers. The creamery burned in 1896 and was rebuilt the next year. The Pioneer Creamery, built in 1889 and located at Arlynda, was the first creamery in the area.

The Ferndale Creamery was built in 1891 on Centerville Road, four miles west of Ferndale. The oldest incorporated creamery in the area, it shipped butter to San Francisco from Port Kenyon, packed in boxes and kegs. It was established by Jacob Rasmussen, E.C. Ericksen, P.J. Petersen, L. Petersen, and other dairymen in the area.

Anna Nissen Jacobsen, a native of Denmark, married her countryman, Julius P. Jacobsen. They became pioneers of the Ferndale dairy industry, moving down to Centerville from Bear River Ridge in 1874. Anna Jacobsen was also an early director of the Ferndale Creamery. Their children were Peter, Annie (Mrs. Jeppe Jespersen), Emma, Ella, and James.

The Central Creamery was established in 1904, occupying the former Ferndale Mechanical Shop building on the north end of Main Street. Dry milk was manufactured there by Aage Jensen and Chester E. Gray, who invented a dry milk spray process. Central also merged with other small creameries in the area. Dairymen who shipped to Central received a 2¢ a pound premium, and were required to meet stringent regulations governing the handling of their milk.

Humboldt Creamery Association, the only remaining creamery still operating in the Ferndale area, was organized by Peter Philipsen in 1928 and built at Fernbridge in 1929. It began operations in 1930, and the cooperative was accepted into the Challenge Cream and Butter Association. The first president of the association was Hans Holgersen; Peter Philipsen was superintendent and general manager. The plant processes fluid milk and butter.

The present Humboldt Creamery Association plant has been enlarged and modernized with the addition of a state-of-the-art ice cream plant. It produces fluid milk and powdered milk, which is shipped to food manufacturing plants for making chocolate and other products. The powdered milk is also exported to foreign countries.

Joseph Gamboni, whose ranch is pictured here, was a native of Switzerland. He moved to Waddington in 1912 where he started dairying. With him were his wife, Berri, and three children, Valentine, Josephine (Tonini), and Marie (Keller). Joseph Gamboni, Valentine's son, and his wife, Rita, later operated the ranch.

The Vinum farm was located at the south end of Francis Street in 1912 on the former Francis property. Rigmore Vinum stands on the bridge over Francis Creek, and her brother Andrew, in his overalls, stands directly behind her and the cows. The second Francis Francis home is nearby, and his farm was called Brook-Dale.

51

Dairymen and their families gather for a Dairymen's banquet at the Portuguese Hall about 1948. Ferndale is very important to ranchers in the area, and ranchers have contributed much to Ferndale's heritage and economy. One can still see tractors rolling down Main Street and pickup trucks with livestock trailers sporting bumper stickers that say, "Ferndale is a Cow Town."

Four

TRANSPORTATION

The first means of transportation in the valley was by foot on trails used by the Indians. Boats were also used to reach Ferndale via the Eel and Salt Rivers and Francis Creek. The Shaw brothers eventually cut a road through the thick ferns and undergrowth to Salt River to enable them to deliver supplies and ship out produce. This photo shows an Indian trail behind Barber Creek at Grizzly Bluff.

The Wildcat Road, pictured here with a view toward Ferndale, was built to connect Ferndale with the hilly Mattole region to the south. Homesteaders and ranchers were thus able to travel and ship products more easily. In 1871 a daily stage began operation between Eureka and Petrolia by way of Table Bluff, Ferndale, and Centerville.

The American Stage Company began service in 1885 and ran between Ferndale and Singley Station, meeting the Eel River and Eureka Railroad, which was a one-and-a-half hour ride to Eureka. Brice and Robarts were the Ferndale agents for the railroad. The first stage line was inaugurated in 1862 and ran between Eureka and Centerville. As more and better roads were built other stage routes followed.

54

After the 1875 fire, the post office was rebuilt next to the Ferndale Hotel, and remained there from 1878 until 1882. A corner of the building can be seen in this photograph at far right, which shows a U.S. Mail delivery stage. In 1878 a daily mail stage ran between Ferndale and Eureka, connecting there with the overland route to San Francisco. In 1884 the Eureka-to-San Francisco mail stage made a stop in Ferndale, with a total travel time of 80 hours and a fare of $20.

George Brice was proprietor or partner in various stage lines and owned a livery stable in Ferndale. He was married to Clara Francis, daughter of Francis Francis. Clara was the first white child born in Ferndale. Shown above is G.M. Brice's stagecoach in 1909.

Letha Brice Shaw is ready to drive away in G.M. Brice's first motor stage, purchased in 1911. Brice's stages ran to Petrolia and Singley.

One of Mr. Brice's unique auto stages is shown parked in front of the Ivanhoe Hotel in 1915. Some of the passengers on board are Mr. Hansen, Harold Francis, Gwen Brice Grinsell, Grace Francis, William McCann, and Mr. Calanchini.

Andrew Sharkey was a stage driver for George Brice for many years. He is shown here with a 1911 or 1912 Pierce Arrow.

A team of horses is pulling a wagon with a tank, either oil or water, at the corner of Ocean Avenue and Main Street in front of the Ferndale Hotel.

This wagon is loaded with posts that were probably used for building fences in the Ferndale area.

A ferry across the Eel River at Singley was first operated in 1861 by William Bradford to carry people, livestock, merchandise, and produce to and from Ferndale and the valley. It was operated at various times by other persons, including George Singley from 1876 to 1880. When Singley's Station was built in 1885, the stage ran on schedules to connect with the train. In 1891 a steam winch moved the ferry, and a pontoon bridge was used in the summer.

Ferndalers had been petitioning the Humboldt County Board of Supervisors since 1893 for a bridge across the Eel River. Supervisor George Hindley led the battle. Bids were finally let out to build the bridge in 1910. Work began March 20, 1910, and was completed November 8, 1911. Fernbridge was constructed of reinforced concrete because buildings of that material had withstood earthquake damage in San Francisco. The $245,967 cost of construction had been paid by the time it was finished. The view of the bridge shown above faces east toward Singley Station (Fernbridge). In the photo below, construction cabins are shown on the east side of the bridge, which is nearing completion. Wooden approach supports were replaced by concrete supports in the 1920s.

Fernbridge has survived many challenges, including a proposal by Cal Trans to replace it with a modern bridge, which failed because of protests from local bridge supporters. It has withstood devastating floods, including the flood of 1964. At that time Fernbridge became the only means of travel to the south as larger, newer bridges were washed out, and the route over Fernbridge through the valley and up the Blue Slide Road was used as a detour for Highway 101. It is truly the "Queen of the Bridges."

This sign stood at the east end of Fernbridge from the 1920s until the 1930s. It was moved to the bottom of Wildcat Road on Ocean Avenue in Ferndale when the road crossing Fernbridge became a state highway.

60

The steamer *Argo* served Port Kenyon from the late 1890s until 1908. She made weekly trips, transporting goods between Port Kenyon and San Francisco, a 24-hour run. The first steamer to serve Port Kenyon was the *Thomas Whitelaw*, commissioned by J.G. Kenyon in 1878. Some of the outgoing cargo from Port Kenyon included grain, potatoes, butter, hides, salmon, and wool. Incoming cargo included merchandise for local stores, household items, liquor, furniture, and other goods for Eel River Valley residents. J.M. Eddy, in the 1893 booklet *In the Redwood's Realm*, described Port Kenyon commerce by noting, "The golden butter flows out, and the golden coin flows in." Shipping finally ceased at Port Kenyon around 1908 due to delays at the mouth of the Eel River caused by shoaling. Goods spoiled during the long wait. As Humboldt Bay developed, it replaced Port Kenyon as the major port in the area. Below is an *Argo* invoice for the Waddington Store.

A wagon hauls lumber down Main Street, with the White Front Store, the Ferndale Market, and Rings Drug Store in the background. The Enterprise lumber mill, built and operated by C.C. Dennis and D.R. Roberts in 1877, stood on the west bank of the Salt River, one mile from Port Kenyon. It was also a grist mill. Redwood and spruce logs were cut for butter box and building lumber, from which several of the homes and barns in the area were built.

The first motorized milk truck in America, manufactured by the Jensen Machine Company in Eureka, was put into service by the Central Creamery in 1914. It was a Pierce Arrow truck with a copper-lined milk tank.

The Barber family tours Grizzly Bluff in their first car, a 1911 Cadillac. In the car are Gardner, Annie, and Emma Barber.

Jim and Anna Lawson are pictured in their first car, a 1911 or 1912 REO. Mr. Lawson was born in Scotland in 1851 and immigrated to the United States in 1853, arriving in California in 1856. In 1875 he was ranching at Grizzly Bluff on Lawson Lane. He managed Grizzly Bluff Creamery and became a trustee of Grizzly Bluff School.

The children of Port Kenyon School are seen here traveling to a picnic in a grove near Fernbridge about 1913. The driver was Claude Sweet, and the horses, Maude and Queen, were from the Occidental Ranch.

Five

BUTTERFAT PALACES AND BUSINESSES

In 1848 Sam Brannan reportedly ran through the streets of San Francisco crying, "Gold! Gold from the American River!" Ferndalers could have sent an agent down south to shout, "Butter! Butter from the Eel River Valley!" because butter was as good as gold to them. The little town that developed to serve the needs of the local dairy farmers became so prosperous that Ferndale was known as the "Cream City," and her magnificent Victorian homes were being referred to as "Butterfat Palaces." Shown here is the Van Ness Avenue home of Mary Russ and her husband, James T. Robarts, known as "The Maples."

Not every house in Ferndale was a Butterfat Palace, nor were they built in any particular style. This plain cottage at 455 Brown Street has molded window caps and unusual open posts on the small front porch. The house was only 70 steps down the wooden sidewalk from Main Street.

A common type of vernacular house was front-gabled with a side wing. The broken pediment on the gable and the decorative posts and porch railing add subdued touches to this house, which stood at the corner of Main and Washington Streets until it was moved in 1929.

Ferndale has only one French Second Empire residence, the Alford-Nielson home, built in the business district in 1877. It has survived two rude shocks. In 1893, it was moved from 421 to 1299 Main Street. Ninety-nine years later, it fell off its footing in the earthquake of 1992.

The large colonnaded front porch, decorative roof brackets, and square shape mark the P.F. Hart house as Italianate in style. The house served the town as Dr. Breuner's hospital from 1915 to 1920. The Ferndale Library, built in 1910, can be seen just to the left of the gabled C.H. Doe home next door.

The home built by Dr. H.J. Ring at the corner of Brown and Berding Streets still dazzles visitors and residents today with its bright color scheme and elegant formal gardens.

The "Skim Milk House" was the nickname given to the Frands Wilhelm Andreasen home in Port Kenyon. Andreasen, a Dane, purchased skim milk and fed it to his pigs as a sideline to his dairy business. The house was completed in 1901, but the family lived there for only ten years before moving to Berkeley, where Andreasen worked for the California State Dairy Bureau. The house, with its double parlor, servants' quarters, stained glass, and interior finishing touches, has been lovingly maintained to this day.

There was not one, but two Jeppe Jespersens in Ferndale. Both were from Denmark, and both were dairymen in the Centerville area. Jeppe Madsen Jespersen, who died in 1928, built this magnificent 1898 home on Russ Lane. The house has a turret, finials, bay windows, mixed siding, sunflowers on the gable ornament, and roof cresting. It is the epitome of a Butterfat Palace, and proud of it.

Victorian interiors were usually quite extravagant. Here, in Martin Ericksen's parlor, we find draped tables, a draped chair, a draped piano, family portraits, sentimental prints, two Danish flags, and a pair of antlers over the door. Ericksen was the proprietor of the Red Front Cigar and Notion Store from 1903 to 1908.

Riding into 19th-century Ferndale, you would have found the American Hotel on the west side of the street, shown here at right, and the Ferndale Hotel at the southern end of town. Like any self-respecting small-town hotel, the American offered its patrons a restaurant, saloon, and barber shop. Across the street was C.A. Doe's Ferndale Livery Stable. Across from the Ferndale Hotel was the American Livery Stable. Both stables housed the offices of a veterinary doctor.

Snow is a rare event in Ferndale, and a local photographer sold scenes of a snowy Main Street taken on March 2, 1896. Looking north we see the Ferndale Hotel on the left and Arnold Berding's store on the right. The *Ferndale Enterprise* of March 3rd mentioned two snow-related misadventures: a horse broke from his wagon after being pelted with a snowball, and a gentleman was seen to tip his hat to a "snow lady," which had been built by some little boys.

The Aggeler Brothers' general store has replaced the earlier Arnold Berding establishment at Main Street and Ocean Avenue in this 1908 photograph. Ferndale has acquired a moving picture theatre, which can be seen at the right just past the *Enterprise* office on the east side of Main Street.

Blacksmith T.H. Brown lived in this home, which sits back from 358 Main Street. Brown also owned the double business building next door. Note the wooden plank perpendicular to the wooden sidewalk to help residents navigate Ferndale's muddy main street.

The *Ferndale Enterprise*, Vol. I, No. 1, appeared on Saturday, May 1, 1878, "Devoted to Agriculture, Commerce, Literature, Science, and Art." The editors and proprietors were William G. Jones & Company, specifically the Jones boys, William, James, and Archibald, sons of the local Methodist Episcopal minister. Terms were given as "$3.00 per annum; $1.00 three months-invariably in advance."

Washing and Ironing

—BY—

SOM LEE,

Done in the best style and

AT THE LOWEST LIVING RATES.

Try him and you will be satisfied.

Frances Street, in rear of Pioneer Livery Stable.

FERNDALE, CAL.   my11tf

Som Lee advertises his laundry service "at the lowest living rates" in the first issue of the *Ferndale Enterprise*. Ferndale had occasional Chinese communities over the years, including work crews for the roads, waterworks and fish canneries at Port Kenyon.

The Ferndale Brick Yard provided bricks for Ferndale's two brick stores, the reservoir, and innumerable chimneys around town. For unknown reasons it became a popular site for young folks' dances and parties.

FERNDALE ✻ RESTAURANT

Meals at all Hours.

Board and Lodging.

Fred Rosen, Prop'r.   -   -   -   Ferndale, Cal.

Fred Rosen's Ferndale Restaurant, located in the old Gilt Edge Hotel, advertised "Meals at all Hours," and "Board and Lodging." The hotel, long gone, is now the site of the Ferndale municipal parking lot. (Courtesy of Gordon Green.)

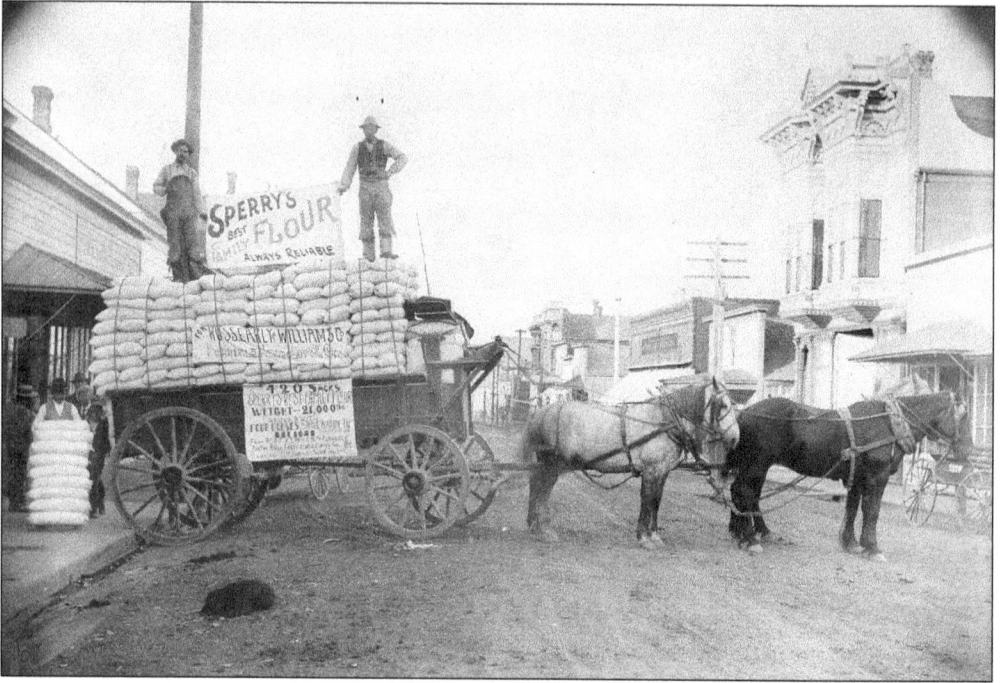

The Sperry's Best Family Flour Company ("Always Reliable") delivers 420 sacks of flour weighing 21,000 pounds to Russ, Early, and Williams Company on August 12, 1896. The teamsters from Port Kenyon were C.A. Bartlett and William Smiley. These facts, advertised on three separate signs, failed to impress the dog sleeping below them.

From 1876 until today there has been a meat market at 376 Main Street. In this 1896 photograph a wagon is either picking up or delivering a carcass to proprietor Z.B. Patrick. Ring's Drug Store can be seen under construction next door.

George Williams built these two eclectic buildings, adorned with Italianate brackets and Stick-Eastlake features on the upper residential stories. Burrill's Candy Kitchen, to the left, later became the Red Star Clothing Company. Kausen and Williams's Hardware Store, to the right, stood in bay-windowed glory until the top two stories had to be taken down after earthquake damage in 1954.

An unblinking eye and a giant stem-wind watch serve to advertise A.P. Winslow's watchmaker and optical shop just to the left of the Brick Store (also known as the Russ, Early & Williams Building), *c.* 1904.

The *Classified Business Directory of Ferndale* in 1898 lists 21 blacksmith establishments. Fred Cruikshanks, seen here at left, was working out of the Henry Hall shop on Main Street at that time, a few steps north of Washington Street.

Charles Wilkinson, known as "Dad," was still a working blacksmith at the time of his death in 1913 at age 81.

Henry Ott called his place of business the Grey Horse Harness Shop, and here the grey horse referred to stands at the back. Ott moved into the south half of the newly constructed meat market building, wallpaper and all. In later years the harnessmaker could be found selling gloves and dusters and repairing automobile tops.

From 1908 to 1910, J.N. Jensen kept a painting business on Shaw Avenue. The wooden facade of R.A. Simpson's Mechanical Shop, to the right, can still be seen today behind the stucco addition to Valley Lumber & Millwork.

Martin Ericksen ran the Red Front Cigar and Notion Store from 1903 to 1908. Martin offered candy, to the left, and cigars, to the right, and between them stands his famous peanut-roasting cart. Two signs can be seen on the rear wall exhorting customers to save the cigar bands.

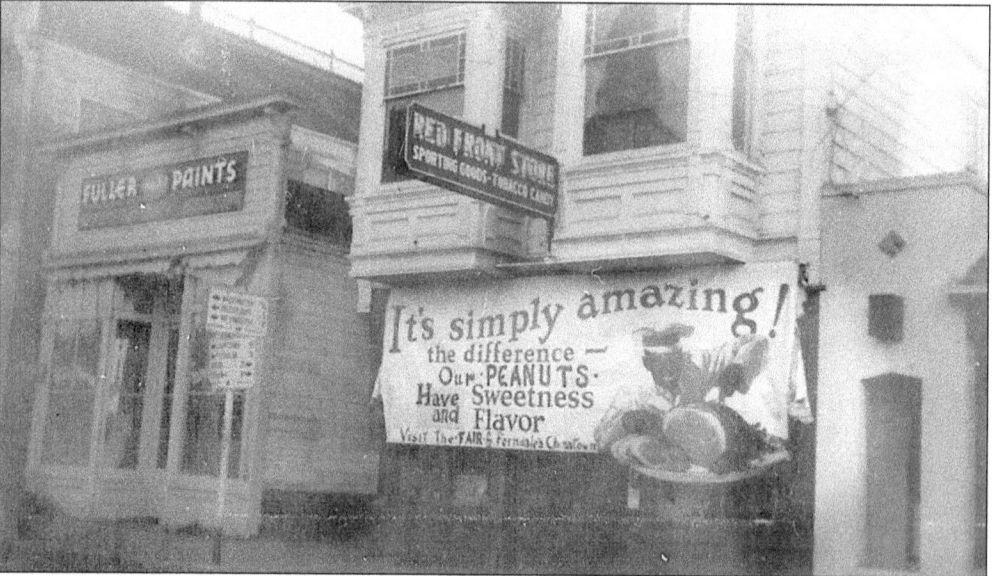

Ferndale has had a Red Front Store, a White Front Store, and a Blue Front Store. Here is the Red Front Store, featuring a banner that indicates that it is still immensely proud of its peanuts. The Kemp building, finished in stucco, is seen to the right.

A portrait of Joseph Russ looks down upon the office of the Russ-Williams Banking Company, located in the Russ, Early & Williams Building, also known as the Brick Store.

Miners, but "No Minors," were allowed at the Palace Saloon, according to a sign over the door. Owned and operated by Mike Donnelly, the saloon had a four-towel, three-spittoon bar. The Grill Room was run by proprietor Ernest Dunn.

Peter Oluf Andreasen built this large commercial complex, the Ferndale Mechanical Shop at Milton and Main Streets in 1894. Peter is shown here at far right with his crew and his two small children. The shop manufactured Andreasen's patented butter molding and cutting machine.

Andreasen, on the left, stands by one of his other manufactured products, the Pacific Butter Box. R.A. Simpson of Ferndale, Andreasen's rival in the mechanical shop line, patented an Improved Creamery Butter Cutter, a Baby Butter Cutter, and the Indestructible Butter Box in 1895.

Six

SOCIAL AND SERVICE ORGANIZATIONS

Thirty subscribers organized the Ferndale Park and Driving Association in 1891, leasing a half-mile racecourse and starting out with a full season of racing, trotting, pacing, and wagering. W.B. Alford, one of the original stockholders, is shown here in his sulky. Today, the estimable Ferndale Jockey Club works to keep the tradition of horse racing alive at the Humboldt County Fair.

Luther Michael, local physician, photographer, fisherman, and dahlia grower, poses for his portrait in the uniform of the Knights Templar, a Masonic order.

Frank Luther (king), Will Dinsmore (high priest), and Dr. Sidney Swift (scribe) led Ferndale's Royal Arch Masons in 1897. (Andrew Genzoli Collection, courtesy of Humboldt State University.)

Ferndale's Civil War veterans would gather for annual campfire meetings so they could enjoy reveille, drill, parade march, target shooting, and hardtack once again. Ferndaler Charles B. Hart, fifth from the left, was famous for having stood guard at the bier of assassinated president Abraham Lincoln.

The Anderson Post No. 21, Grand Army of the Republic, invited wives and children to this particular camp-out. (Andrew Genzoli Collection, courtesy of Humboldt State University.)

The Knights of Pythias celebrate the opening of the Pythian Castle with a grand parade on May 8, 1896. The building had electricity and arc lighting. A carbon arc streetlight can be seen at the intersection of Main Street and Shaw Avenue.

Sallie Shortribs and Saphronia Sassafras were among the featured performers when the Fernleaf Temple of the Rathbone Sisters put on their minstrel show in 1908. The Rathbone Sisters were the ladies auxiliary of the Knights of Pythias.

Ferndale had a brass band for concerts, a string band for dances, and a cornet band for parades. Here the members of the Ferndale Cornet Band, showing off their new uniforms, gather in front of the Russ Building along with a number of little boys in short pants and caps.

The International Order of Good Templars was an organization that gathered together in large numbers for the express purpose of abstaining from intoxicating drink. The Ferndale Lodge sits, stands, and reclines for its portrait in 1895.

Woodmen of the World hitch up their oxen and wooden cabin float for the Fourth of July parade in 1898. The Woodmen were a fraternal, insurance, and burial society. They were partial to granite gravestones carved to look like tree branches and inscribed, "Here Lies a Woodman of the World."

The Native Daughters of the Golden West seem to be running a babysitting service at the Humboldt County Fair. The two ladies in dark dresses, top left and right, are definitely Native Daughters. They are Amelia Francis Robarts and Clara Francis Brice, native Ferndalers born in 1859 and 1858, respectively.

The Reverend Arthur B. Roberts of the Congregational Church had an extensive program of activities for Ferndale boys and girls. The boys Military and Athletic Association Band marched in local parades. The Girls Club, shown here with fencing foils in hand, solemnly poses at the corner of Fifth Street and Ocean Avenue.

The Hupa Tribe of Redmen of Eureka—or so they called themselves—were guest participants in the Ferndale Fourth of July parade in 1911. The gentlemen in the front row are the Ivanhoes, Ferndale's baseball team. Star player Joe Oeschger, second from the right, went on to set a major league record when he pitched a 26-inning game in 1920 for the Boston Braves.

The Village Club, established in 1906, is a ladies social, cultural, and philanthropic organization. Here the Village Club members entertain each other with a musical frenzy of some sort.

For 30 years the Village Club met in their clubhouse at 834 Main Street. In 1967 the building was donated to Ferndale for use as a city hall, but the ladies continue to meet in the building, which still features kitchen and parlor facilities that lend themselves to gracious entertaining.

Ferndale's Portuguese community marches past its hall during a Holy Ghost parade memorialized in this photo. The Holy Ghost celebration, with its Mass, dinner, banners, and queens, has taken place in Ferndale since 1924, the same year that the Portuguese Hall Association purchased Roberts Hall on Ocean Avenue.

Before construction of the Veterans Memorial building on Main Street, the Veterans of Foreign Wars met in the front parlor of the Dr. Ring home on Berding Street. Ampelio Tunzini, Andy Genzoli, and Elvin Coppini are shown here participating in a ceremony. In World War I Ferndale lost 9 servicemen, 19 were lost in World War II, with 1 more in the Korean War, and 5 in Vietnam. Their names are inscribed on the roll of honor in front of the Veterans Building.

The establishment of the Ferndale Museum was a four-year project, from "Lay Plans for Local Museum," (*Ferndale Enterprise,* May 1, 1975), to "Ferndale Museum a Reality," (*Ferndale Enterprise,* October 4, 1979). The County Maintenance Barn on Shaw Avenue was the chosen site for the museum.

Clubs, foundations, carpenters, decorators, cookie bakers—volunteers all—built the Ferndale Museum, and a large number of faithful volunteers continue to ensure its existence today.

Seven

SPECIAL EVENTS

Like most towns in America, Ferndale has a tradition of celebrating holidays and anniversaries with parades and festivities. Here five women from Grizzly Bluff have boarded a patriotically festooned wagon drawn by a two-horse team en route to a turn of the century Fourth of July parade, complete with coachman and grooms.

A major event in village history was the ceremony for the first graduating class of the Ferndale Union High School in 1907. From left to right are Florence Buttle, Beatrice Faulkner, Professor W.H. Van Horn (principal), John Lund, Teresa McDonough, and Elinor Varley. The initials FUHS can be discerned on the banner at the back of the dais.

Lucille Robarts Lanini, granddaughter of Grace Francis, and Marian Shaw Bartlett, granddaughter of Isabella Shaw, are shown dressed in authentic period clothing, parasol and bonnets included, for the celebration of Ferndale's centennial in 1952. The wheelchair with its original occupant is shown on page 15. The ladies are posed in front of the *Ferndale Enterprise* office.

One of the highlights of the 1952 Ferndale centennial celebration was this multi-tiered cake created by the Ferndale Bakery under the direction of Primo Marca, seen just to the right behind the cake. The large medallion on the base features the ferns that gave the town its name. Standing beside the cake on the mobile platform is Irene Marca, Primo's wife.

Just one year later, in 1953, Humboldt County made its centennial cake that much greater, higher, and more elaborate than Ferndale's. This incredible edible work of art, displayed here at the Humboldt County Fairground in Ferndale, weighed one ton and involved considerable engineering expertise from its creator, Primo Marca. The medallions feature a lighthouse and a shield.

A 1911 Fourth of July pony cart entry, bunting threading its wheels, is driven by Muriel Garrett, at front in center, who earned the honor by being three years older than Grace Lawson, at left, and Emma Donely, at right. Evelyn Slingsby, in back, is holding the flag. Obscured by the second flag are Agnes and Frank Slingsby. Lena Rutledge Lawson, in flowered hat, and her sister Grace supervise from the boardwalk.

At 2 a.m. on Armistice Day, the town fire siren announced to Ferndale that World War I was over. People poured into the streets to celebrate, and a monster parade of tooting cars cruised the county all day. In this photograph, a procession of Grizzly Bluff residents pauses on the outskirts of town to put on gauze masks, which were required by law on the streets of Ferndale. The second great tragedy of 1918 was the Spanish influenza epidemic raging at that time.

Ferndale has been the permanent site of the Humboldt County Fair since 1896. By 1900, events included cattle lassoing, a ladies bicycle race, horse racing, horse tournaments, free band concerts, and a fair ball on the final night. Betting on horse races was illegal then, and only in 1935 when pari-mutuel wagering was allowed did the spectator sport become the major attraction it is today. In 1938 a new grandstand and other racing facilities were added. In 1949 a small-scale replica of the old Cape Mendocino Lighthouse, containing its original 1868 Fresnel lens, was moved to the fairgrounds and still stands in welcome at the main entrance. Centerville's "little red schoolhouse," built in 1880, was also moved to the fairgrounds, where it serves as a museum.

Memorial Day has a two-fold emphasis: providing the spectacle of a patriotic parade and the solemnity of a religious service at the Ferndale Cemetery. In the 1907 picture above, students and teachers of the local school march in their Sunday best, with elaborately decorated hats, carrying flowers along Ocean Avenue, as townsfolk line the route. In the scene below, a gunfire salute to deceased veterans marks the ceremony in the cemetery, while members of a fraternal order and a small crowd observe.

This funeral procession in 1892 for J.D. Ferrill, justice of the peace, gives an indication of the respect the people of Ferndale felt for their dignitaries. Note the plumes on the horse-drawn hearse, the numerous carriages riding in the procession, and the wagons drawn respectfully to the side. A banner for presidential candidates Benjamin Harrison and Whitelaw Reid can be seen in the background, strung across Main Street.

The Holy Ghost Festival is a religious tradition honoring the sixth Queen Isabella of Portugal. It has been observed for six centuries in the Azores and was brought here by Portuguese immigrants at the turn of the 20th century. A young woman elected to represent the Queen, is shown with her attendants, followed by the "Little Queen" and entourage. The annual parade marches from Portuguese Hall to Assumption Church.

The internationally known Kinetic Sculpture Race originated in Ferndale in 1969 when local sculptor and art dealer Hobart Brown was carried away by artistic zeal while repairing his son's tricycle. The resulting seven-foot structure attracted attention, and the idea of the Kinetic Sculpture Race was born. Many remarkable entries are on display at the Kinetic Sculpture Museum on Main Street. Brown is shown here with his son Justin.

Ferndale's famous Sitka spruce, the tallest living Christmas tree in the country at approximately 150 feet, rises high above Main Street today. When the Volunteer Fire Department decorates the tree each year with hundreds of lights, it can be seen for miles. Since 1934 a tree lighting Ceremony has been held on the first Sunday in December, with refreshments, a band, and carolers. The tree is pictured here after a rare snowfall. (Andrew Genzoli Collection, courtesy of Humboldt State University.)

Gertrude Clausen addresses representatives of the Ferndale City Council and local dignitaries on behalf of the Village Club during the Town Hall dedication and transfer of deeds in 1967. In the front row, from left to right, are John Lund, Primo Marca, Elmer Haskins, Karl Brungs, John Trigg, Donna Richardson representing Native Daughters of the Golden West, Assemblyman Frank Belotti, Dora Damon, Congressman Don Clausen, Glenda Miller, Harriet Crane, Lorie Ford, Everett Hall, and Mona Detlefsen.

Ferndale has been the location for three major film productions. *Salem's Lot*, starring James Mason and David Soul, was filmed here in 1979. *Outbreak*, with Dustin Hoffman and Rene Russo, virtually took over the town and employed many residents as extras in 1994, as did *The Majestic*, with Jim Carrey, in 2001. At extreme left is Jerry Lesandro, director of the Ferndale Museum, with actors Lew Ayres and David Soul in a scene from *Salem's Lot*.

An earthquake in 1954 and a major flood in 1955 left Ferndale looking slightly worse for wear. In 1962, *Ferndale Enterprise* editors George and Hazel Waldner raised the issue of the dilapidated appearance of Main Street and spurred a weekend "paint-up," with citizens contributing labor, materials, and equipment. Residents were also energized to restore their Victorian homes. The marked improvement in the city's appearance prompted the city council to adopt a zoning ordinance insisting on conformity to the Victorian theme in the center of town. This ended efforts to modernize old properties, which would have destroyed the period ambience of the town. Today Ferndale is a tourist destination, thanks to its fame as a California Historical Landmark (Number 883) and the placement of the downtown area on the National Register of Historic Places.

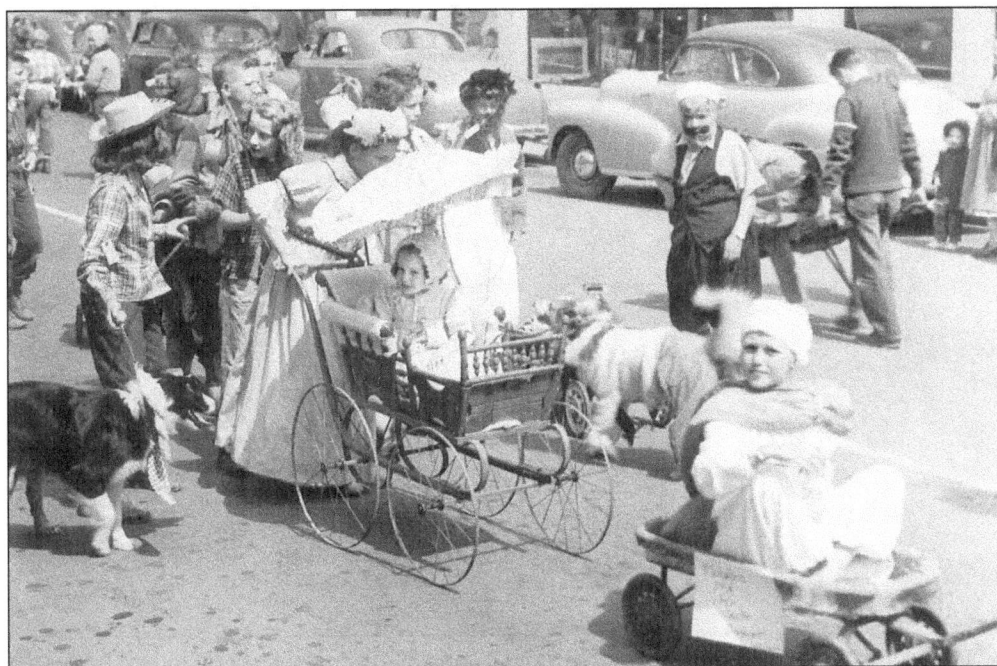

This amusing scene from the 1950s is the Rural Schools Pet Parade. Started by the Ferndale Chamber of Commerce in the 1940s, the annual parade originally included entries from all schools in the area. Today, with the erstwhile rural schools consolidated into the Ferndale Elementary School, it is open to all children, who parade with pets as varied as horses and calves and giant banana slugs. All entrants receive a prize.

Ferndale children are enjoying their traditional noisy Fourth of July ride around town, provided by the Ferndale Volunteer Fire Department. This 1950s photograph shows the department's 1923 American LaFrance fire engine, front left.

War veterans of the town participate in Memorial Day activities, shown here, and in the Fourth of July parade. (Courtesy of The Blacksmith Shop, Ferndale.)

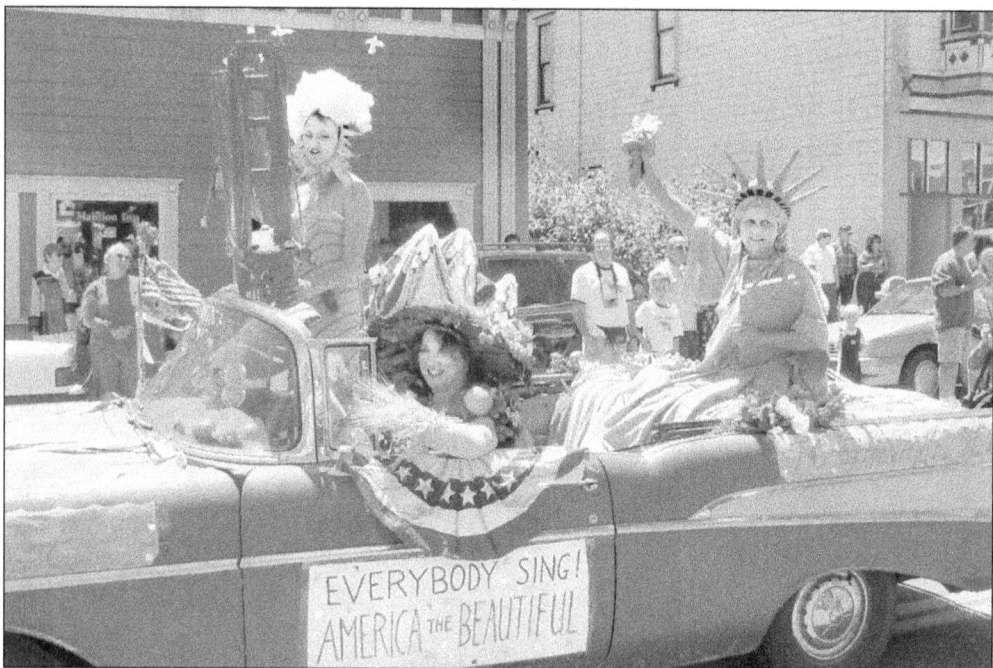

The Ferndale Repertory Theatre sponsors a triple header for the Fourth of July–morning parade, a lunch on the Green, and a band concert in the afternoon. Sisters Carolyn Meade, Ellie Green, and Loretta Huntress, left to right, present "America the Beautiful." Carolyn, holding the Golden Gate Bridge, and Loretta, the Statue of Liberty, represent "from sea to shining sea." Ellie, driving her 1957 Chevrolet convertible, wears "purple mountain majesties" and "amber waves of grain." (Courtesy of The Blacksmith Shop, Ferndale.)

102

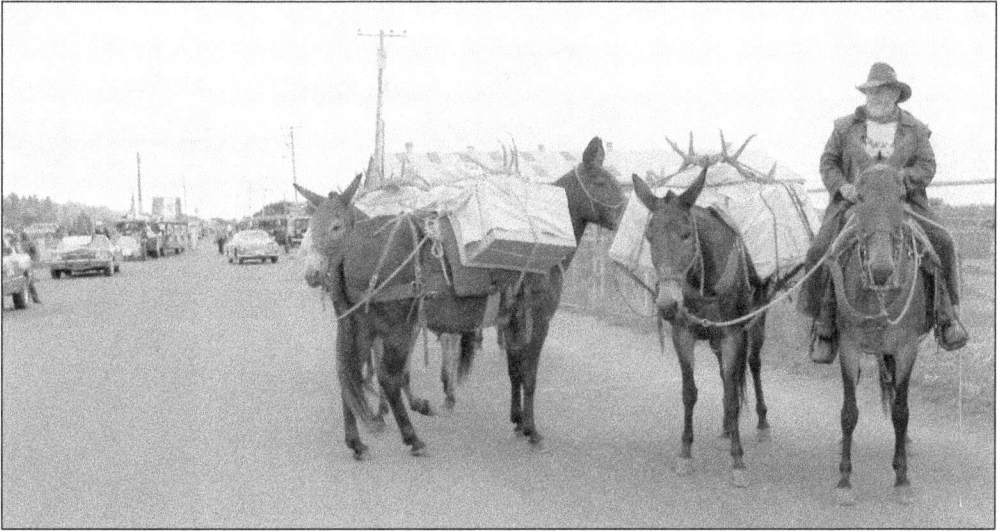

Darrell Polasek readies his pack mules for the Ferndale Sesquicentennial Parade.

Mayor Jeff Farley, standing by the official logo, was emcee for the concluding ceremonies of Ferndale's sesquicentennial celebration held the weekend of August 23 and 24, 2002. Sesquicentennial events included a parade, street dancing, barbecue, art show, window displays, historical bulletin boards, and a trek by land and water from Table Bluff, re-tracing the route of Seth and Stephen Shaw in 1852.

Since 1992, farmers, ranchers, families, businesses, and organizations have been decorating tractors and tractor-drawn wagons with Christmas lights and imaginative seasonal displays for the Ferndale Christmas Lighted Tractor Parade. Each entry is described by announcers on Main Street, and trophies are given for such categories as Most Original, Most Lights, Oldest Tractor, and Best Christmas Theme. People attend from throughout the county and beyond. (Courtesy of Pete and Mary Ann Bansen.)

The interfaith, intergenerational Ferndale Community Choir is a 35-year-old Humboldt County institution. Under the leadership of Betty Diehl, they present concerts at Christmas and Easter, featuring local soloists and instrumental accompaniment. Betty Diehl also directs the Chameleon Singers, an informal vocal group that lends its musical talent to numerous town events throughout the year. (Courtesy of Robin Robin.)

Eight

DISASTERS

Ferndale has endured and survived floods, earthquakes, fires, and shipwrecks from its earliest beginnings. Floods on the Eel River have caused extensive damage to the valley many times. Local Indian legends tell of a very large earthquake 300 years ago, and this has since been documented from geological evidence. Other significant earthquakes have occurred in the Ferndale area since the first settlers came. Fires have taken their toll and ships have sunk and run aground on the treacherous North Coast.

The Shaw family motors out to investigate a flood in the early 1900s. The automobile is a 1906 two-cycle REO. J.A. Shaw is driving with passengers Marion Shaw and Smith Hart, Marion's uncle.

The 1955 flood was the highest documented flood level in history until the 1964 flood. Shown here are rescue worker Ron Smith, at left, and another volunteer helping Dora, Louise, and Charlie Zana out of a boat. The Zanas were rescued from the second floor of their house after escaping through an upstairs window. The house was repaired after the 1955 flood, but the waters rose even higher in 1964, forcing it to be abandoned. Occidental Ranch is seen in the background.

Rescue workers and residents are shown waiting at a submerged road in 1955.

A collapsed barn, still full of hay, floats up beside Fernbridge in 1955.

The December 1964 flood was the worst on record. Unprecedented rain fell from December 1 through December 23. In December 1955, the height of the river reached 27.7 feet at Fernbridge. In 1964 it rose to 29.5 feet. Seven lives and 4,000 animals were lost. Homes, barns, and property were destroyed. Towns were wiped out. People were rescued from the roofs of their homes by helicopter and boat. The water washed away roads and bridges. It is estimated that Humboldt County property sustained $500 million in damage. Farmers, business owners, and residents returned to clean up and rebuild their lives. Roads, bridges, and the railroad were repaired and restored with the fervent wish that no one will ever see a "1,000 year flood" again.

The North Coast of California is at the confluence of the Mendocino Triple Junction, where three plates on the earth's crust meet: the Gorda, the North American, and the Pacific Plates. When these three shift and collide they cause earthquakes. On April 6, 1906, the San Andreas fault ruptured from Santa Cruz as far north as southern Humboldt County, causing devastation in San Francisco and significant damage in the Ferndale and Petrolia areas. Shown here is damage on Main Street in Ferndale.

The badly damaged "White Front" store housed the Boynton and Hall clothing store. The Ferndale fire-bell tower was on top of the building and toppled during the 1906 earthquake. Seen on the side of the building is a sign announcing a sale on April 7th. The building was torn down and replaced by the Ferndale Bank in 1911.

The Pythian Castle, on the corner of Main and Shaw Streets, had three stories, with a dance hall on the top floor, a meeting hall on the second, and Duck Brothers furniture store on the ground level. Badly damaged in the 1906 earthquake it was finally torn down in the 1930s.

Shown here is another view of the 1906 earthquake damage to the Pythian Castle.

The Russ, Early, and Williams store, also known as the Brick Store, was built in 1876. It was a general merchandise store, and suffered heavy damage in the 1906 earthquake when the entire brick front fell off into the street. Having just been remodeled three months previously, it was rebuilt after the quake with a brick façade.

The Valley Grocery occupied the same building as the Russ, Early & Williams store, shown above. On April 25, 1992, three separate earthquakes, centered off Cape Mendocino near Ferndale and Petrolia, again damaged the store. They were recorded as a 7.1 on the Richter scale, followed by a 6.6 earthquake early the next morning, and finally a 6.7 earthquake. The grocery store also lost its brick front and had to be rebuilt, but this time without brick.

111

The old Alford-Nielson home, built in 1877, was knocked off its foundation (see early photo, page 67) as were many other older homes in Ferndale. Some of the strongest shaking ever recorded in California was produced by the first 1992 earthquake.

This home on Berding Street was torn apart in the 1992 earthquakes. Many chimneys in town were also lost. Most of the homes that were damaged because of poor foundations were jacked up and placed on new reinforced concrete perimeter foundations. Homes and businesses were repaired and strengthened with the hope that all will withstand the next "Big One."

A Bosch Omori seismograph was installed in the town hall on January 25, 1933, by Joseph Bognuda and Horace Winslow. It had been loaned to Mr. Bognuda by the University of California to monitor seismic activity in the area. In the 1950s, the university gave the seismograph to Ferndale, and it is now installed at the Ferndale Museum. A needle records ground movements, their severity, and time on a removable roll, which is changed every 24 hours. Significant readings are kept as a permanent record.

Ferndale has had many fires. One of the worst occurred on September 6, 1875. The fire started at the Ferndale Hotel, and eventually destroyed it as well as the Dodge, Russ & Company store and the Ferndale Grange Association store. The Roberts Livery Stable and Berding's General Merchandise store were saved. The photo above shows Ferndale Town Hall, the large two-story building at right center. The building also housed the Good Templar Hall upstairs, as well as the fire engine and jail. On May 30, 1893, Ferndale Town Hall was destroyed by an arson fire originating in the house of Edna Gardner, who was operating a house of prostitution next door. Gardner's house had been the target of some very angry women residents, who tried to knock it off its foundation as it was being built. After her house burned, Edna Gardner left town. No one was ever found responsible for the fire.

Fires have always been a great threat to Ferndale because many of the older buildings are connected to one another through the attics. The Ferndale Volunteer Fire Department always responds rapidly and has kept fire damage to the town under control.

The Codoni Apartments above the post office were ruined by smoke and water damage in this December 4, 1950 fire, but the *Ferndale Enterprise* reported that the excellent work of the fire department saved the Christmas mail.

On January 5, 1860, the paddle wheel steamer, *Northerner,* carrying 53 passengers, 53 crew members, and cargo, struck a rock off Cape Mendocino. Not realizing the extent of the damage, Capt. William Dall continued north. As a storm came up, the ship began taking on water and commenced firing distress signals, which were heard at Humboldt Bay. The seas became rougher and the winds stronger, and the ship beached about one mile south of Centerville. A line was brought to shore and small boats launched. Two capsized, throwing passengers overboard. Others jumped overboard as the ship broke up. Seventeen passengers and 21 crew members died. Bodies that were recovered were buried in a pit on Centerville Beach. Salvaged merchandise was sold at auction at Berding's Store in Centerville. The Native Sons of the Golden West erected this cross above the beach in 1921. Although toppled by the 1992 earthquake, it was restored and rededicated on February 16, 1995.

Nine

PEOPLE OF THE VALLEY

Constance Aggeler was born on the Island in 1896. According to her obituary, she was the first child baptized in the new Assumption Catholic Church.

Master Lee Collins in his Zouave suit couldn't look more fetching in this 1896 studio portrait.

Little Warren Ott, proud owner of a velocipede, an early version of the bicycle, recovers in a hip-to-ankle cast from his collision with a delivery wagon in 1908.

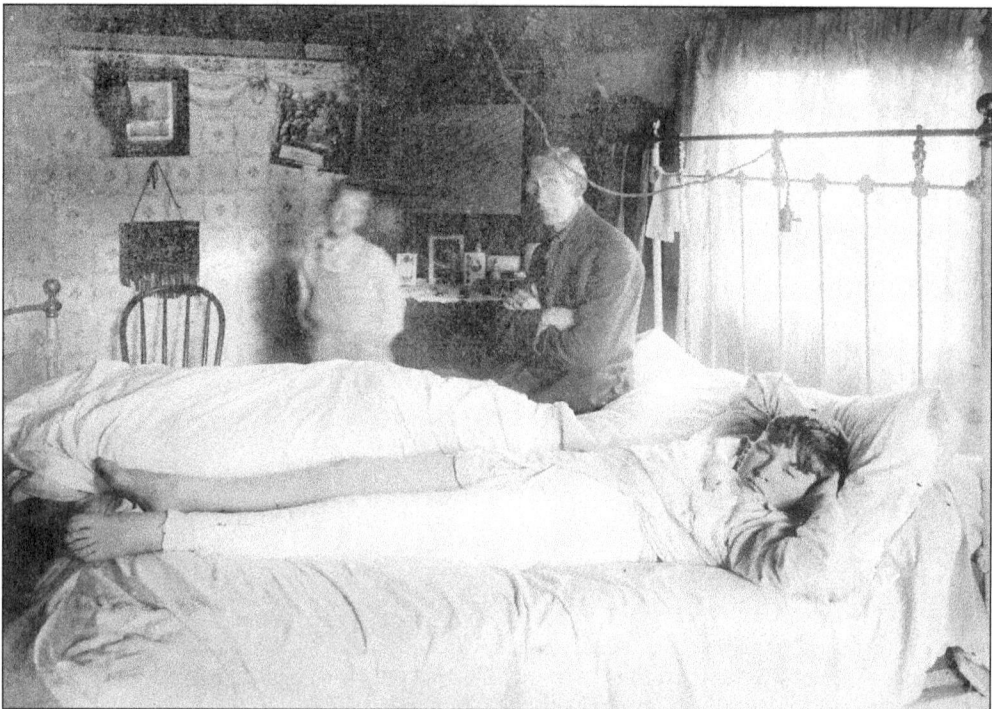

When Francis Francis began selling his land for commercial development in Ferndale, Frederick Cassins was his first buyer in June 1868. Cassins, shown here, purchased six acres at the crossroads corner, today's Ocean Avenue and Main Street, and put up Cassins' Hotel, which he sold to David Roberts in 1872.

Aage Jensen established the Central Creamery in 1904. In 1913 he and C.E. Gray patented a dry-milk process and brought a new industry to Humboldt County.

Frank Alford, early Ferndale physician, took a couple of years out of his professional career to run the Ferndale Enterprise from 1880 to 1883. His medical career spanned 20 years in Ferndale. The doctor is seen in his parlor with wife, Mary, and daughter Bertha.

In its 126 years of existence, the *Ferndale Enterprise* has had five women editors: Hazel Waldner (1977), Marilyn Lidner (1980), Elizabeth Poston McHarry (1982), Marsha van de Berg (1995), and Caroline Titus (1996). Hazel Waldner, shown here, took over editorship of the paper during World War II, in the absence of her husband, George. Hazel's two-and-a-half-inch headline and ten-inch Statue of Liberty, both in bright red, announcing the end of the war, earned her a California Newspaper Publishers Award.

Rev. Richard Rhodda and his wife served the Methodist Episcopal congregations of Ferndale and Grizzly Bluff from 1894 to 1897.

Fr. Joseph Crowley, S.J., attended St. Mary's Convent School in Ferndale. He was ordained in St. Louis in 1918 and became a teacher at Santa Clara University. His parents, John and Johanna Crowley, sold part of their property just east of the Ferndale city limits for a Catholic Cemetery in 1884.

Sarah Locke poses with her diploma from San Jose Normal School in 1880. Her first job was at the Centerville School, and in 1882 she married William T. Smith. Their daughter Gertrude attended the new Arcata Normal School and also became a local teacher.

Abigail Dean Chapman Cardozo Hayes of Grizzly Bluff was a dairywoman and storekeeper who became famous for her flair for photography. She kept a studio in Ferndale for ten years before moving to Oakland with her third husband and taking up a new art form—ceramic painting.

Clark Mason Smith was a man of many aspects: civic official, fraternal brother, captain of the town baseball team, undertaker, and member of the Bon Ton Social Club.

Four downtown gents pause in front of a hardware store with their purchases. Behind them is a poster for Ferndale's first Aviation Meet at the Fair Grounds in May of 1912. (Andrew Genzoli Collection, courtesy of Humboldt State University.)

Elizabeth and George Slingsby relax with the newspaper and their rocking chairs. Elizabeth and George ran a dairy and had 12 children.

James Slingsby, Waddington blacksmith, was the son of George and Elizabeth, shown above. His wife, Della Chapman, artist and dressmaker, was the daughter of Abbie Chapman, artist and photographer. One of Della's paintings of redwoods along a stream hangs in the parlor of the Ferndale Museum.

Ann and William Lytel, natives of Nova Scotia, raised 13 children on their farm on the Island.

The Cornelius Rasmussen family gathers for the wedding of their hired hand, Otto Jespersen, and his bride, Mariane Odgoord, seated in front, on April 26, 1906. They were both Danish immigrants. Christian and Christine Rasmussen, second row, acted as witnesses to the ceremony. Rev. A.H. Jensen of Our Savior's Danish Lutheran Church is in the center of the group.

Reece Cruickshanks was a Ferndale doughboy during World War I.

Some young ladies from Grizzly Bluff knit for the Red Cross during World War I. From left to right are Anne Schortgen, Ruth Church, and Iola Sweet.

Marine Pvt. Stuart Rochqueforte Macklin died at Guadalcanal in 1943 at the age of 19. In the same year, the Stuart Macklin Post 559 of the American Legion was organized in his hometown.

Kenneth Rasmussen of Waddington enlisted in the U.S. Army in 1939. He died in the Philippines in 1942. Ferndale's Veterans of Foreign Wars Post 6353 honors his memory.

The Bertha Russ Lytel Foundation is Ferndale's premier philanthropic organization. Bertha Millicent Russ was the last surviving child of Zipporah and Joseph Russ when she died in 1972 at the age of 98. Her bequest of $4 million to the town of Ferndale has quadrupled in today's dollars, and the Lytel Foundation gives assistance to 40 local worthy causes annually.

Viola Russ McBride was at home on the range and just about everywhere else. She went from Fern Cottage to boarding school to the University of California, Davis (the "University Farm"), where she was a student of agriculture and animal husbandry in 1927. She was an artist and a patron of the arts. She was a landowner and a preserver of Ferndale's historic heritage. Viola Russ McBride continued the traditions of her aunt, Bertha Russ Lytel, and her pioneer grandmother, Zipporah Patrick Russ. Three great ladies—and Ferndale will always be the richer for them. (Courtesy of the McBride family.)

Visit us at
arcadiapublishing.com

www.ingramcontent.com/pod-product-compliance
Lightning Source LLC
Chambersburg PA
CBHW080630110426
42813CB00006B/1646